LARGE

EUCHA

ADORATION

Prayers, Meditations and Devotions

All booklets are published thanks to the generous support of the members of the Catholic Truth Society

CATHOLIC TRUTH SOCIETY
PUBLISHERS TO THE HOLY SEE

CONTENTS

PRAYING WITH THE SAINTS 34

RITE OF EUCHARISTIC EXPOSITION AND BENEDICTION

PRAYING BEFORE THE BLESSED SACRAMENT

Could you not watch with me one hour? (Mt 26:40)

Jesus asked his disciples in the Garden of Gethsemane to watch one hour with him. Eucharistic Adoration is an opportunity to respond to Jesus' request. The devotion of the 'holy hour' before the Blessed Sacrament has through the centuries been a privileged time for Christians to pray and meditate in the very presence of our Lord.

Even if we are unable to find one whole hour, we can still devote what is today called 'quality time' to our relationship with Jesus.

There is no set formula for Eucharistic Adoration. An act of Adoration (e.g. page 48) is a good way o f acknowledging that we are in the presence of God himself. Then, like at Mass, we can say sorry for the sins which have disrupted our relationship with God and neighbour.

During prayer, our minds often become distracted, perhaps we even feel bored. If so, it is helpful to divide the time into reading scripture (pages 17-21), meditation (pages 22-24) and prayer (e.g. the Rosary pages 55-87).

Above all, remember that "the Spirit too comes to our help in our weakness, for, when we do not know how to pray properly, then the Spirit personally makes our petitions for us in sighs that cannot be put into words." (*Rm* 8:26)

THE EUCHARIST

The Eucharist - sharing Christ's one sacrifice

The sacrifice offered by Christ in his death and resurrection was so decisive for the salvation of the human race that Jesus returned to the Father only after he had left us a means of sharing in it. He gave us the Mass as its memorial celebration, which makes Christ's one, definitive redemptive sacrifice always present in time.

The Real Presence of Jesus

This sacrificial presence within the Eucharist is crowned by the reality of his personal presence. Christ is really present in other ways too - in prayer and in the other sacraments - yet in the Eucharist he comes as God and Man, wholly and entirely present. After the consecration the bread and wine cease to exist, so that the adorable body and blood of the Lord Jesus from that moment on are really before us under the sacramental species of bread and wine.

Because the living Jesus is
present in this way, the gift of his
body and blood increases within us
the gift of his Spirit, already poured
out in Baptism and bestowed
as a 'seal' in the sacrament of
Confirmation. By the Eucharist,
Christ continually transforms
us into his own divine likeness
through the Holy Spirit.

The Eucharist is also the pledge
of the future Resurrection, because
the flesh of the Son of Man,
given as Eucharistic food, is his
body in its glorious state after the
Resurrection. Receiving his flesh
and blood means sharing both in

his Resurrection and in the Holy
Spirit who is the foretaste and
pledge of our own Resurrection.

The Eucharist is participation in
the heavenly liturgy of Mary and
all the Saints and angels, a true
glimpse of heaven appearing on
earth. It is a glorious ray of the
heavenly Jerusalem piercing the
clouds of history and lightening
our earthly journey.

The Eucharist builds the Church

We are united with him not only
as individuals but in his body
the Church. The Eucharist both

fully expresses our union as Christ's Church both fostering and promoting the growth of the Church on earth.

This is why sharing in the Sunday liturgy is so essential to the Christian life. In the Eucharist we not only share in the Lord's passion and death we also partake of his risen body and blood. Thus we become what we truly are: the body of Christ.

This awesome reality of his presence in the Eucharist requires that we continue Eucharistic adoration outside the Mass, in exposition of the Blessed

Sacrament and in prayer of adoration before the tabernacle.

Precisely because of the communal nature of the Eucharist, those not in full communion with the Church are not, except in certain extraordinary circumstances, to receive communion within a Catholic liturgy; nor are Catholics permitted to receive communion within liturgies whose ministers are not validly ordained.

THE WORD OF GOD

The Table of the Word and the
Table of the Sacrament are
intimately connected. The Holy
Scriptures proclaim Christ and the
salvation he offers. They present an
intimate account of how Jesus ate
and drank with his disciples before
his Passion.

But the institution of the
Eucharist did not take place in a
vacuum. The context of the Last
Supper was the Passover, a ritual
meal in which the Jews celebrate

their liberation from slavery in Egypt as recounted in the book of Exodus. The first Christians who feasted upon the Risen Christ at the breaking of bread understood that Jesus had become their Passover. This is why we can say, "Every Mass is a mini-Easter." In many parts of the Bible, the imagery used to describe salvation is rich in allusions to feasting. The promised kingdom would be full of the finest wheat, and new wine.

FOUR THEMES FOR ADORATION

1. God will provide
- *Jn* 6:26-35

Then they said to him, 'What must we do if we are to do the works that God wants?' Jesus gave them this answer, 'This is working for God: you must believe in the one he has sent'.

So they said, 'What sign will you give to show us that we should believe in you? What work will you do? Our fathers had manna to eat in

the desert; as scripture says:
He gave them bread from heaven
to eat'.

Jesus answered: 'I tell you most
solemnly, it was not Moses who
gave you bread from heaven, it is
my Father who gives you the bread
from heaven, the true bread; for the
bread of God is that which comes
down from heaven and gives life to
the world'.

'Sir,' they said 'give us that bread
always.' Jesus answered:

'I am the bread of life.

He who comes to me will never
be hungry; he who believes in me
will never thirst.

2. The Eucharist: Sacrament of Unity - *1 Co* 10:16-17

The blessing-cup that we bless is a communion with the blood of Christ, and the bread that we break is a communion with the body of Christ.

The fact that there is only one loaf means that, though there are many of us, we form a single body because we all have a share in this one loaf.

3. The Eucharist: Foretaste of heavenly glory - *Rv* 3:20-21

Look, I am standing at the door, knocking. If one of you hears me calling and opens the door, I will come in to share his meal, side by side with him. Those who prove victorious I will allow to share my throne, just as I was victorious myself and took my place with my Father on his throne.

4. The Institution of the Eucharist - *1 Co* 11:23-26

For this is what I received from the Lord, and in turn passed on to you: that on the same night that he was betrayed, the Lord Jesus took some bread, and thanked God for it and broke it, and he said, 'This is my body, which is for you; do this as a memorial of me'. In the same way he took the cup after supper, and said, 'This cup is the new covenant in my blood. Whenever you drink it, do this as a memorial of me.' Until the Lord comes, therefore, every time you eat this bread and drink this cup, you are proclaiming his death.

MEDITATIONS

These are texts uttered slowly and thoughtfully out of a background of silence. They are especially effective when used in a quiet church after silent prayer or meditation.

The new life

Lord Jesus,
you give us bread which is
    your body,
you give us wine which is
    your blood
to feed and strengthen us
on our way through life.

Help us to appreciate this gift
    more clearly,
and help us to live the new life your
    won for us
through your saving death
    and resurrection.

Lord, help us

Lord Jesus,
when you come again at the end
    of time,
we shall already know you a little
through the gift of your body which
    you left us.
Help us to be ready …

Anima Christi

Soul of Christ, sanctify me.
Body of Christ, save me.
Blood of Christ, inebriate me.
Water from the side of Christ,
    wash me.
Passion of Christ, strengthen me.
O good Jesu, hear me. Within thy
wounds hide me.
Suffer me not to be separated from
thee. From the malicious enemy,
defend me. In the hour of my death,
call me,
and bid me come to thee.
That with your saints I may praise
thee, for all eternity.
Amen.

PRAYERS AND LITANIES

Act of Adoration

O Jesus, my God, my Creator,
I adore you, because from your
hands I came and with you I am to
be happy for ever. O Jesus, I am
not worthy to receive you, and yet
you have come to me that my poor
heart may learn of you to be meek
and humble. Jesus, I love you; I
love you with all my heart. You
know that I love you, and wish to
love you daily more and more. My
good Jesus, I thank you with all my

heart. How good, how kind you are
to me. Blessed be Jesus in the most
holy Sacrament of the Altar.

Act of Offering

O Jesus, receive my poor offering.
Jesus, you have given yourself
    to me,
and now let me give myself to you:
I give you my body,
    that I may be chaste and pure.
I give you my soul,
    that I may be free from sin.
I give you my heart,
    that I may always love you.
I give you my every breath
    that I shall breathe,
and especially my last.

I give you myself in life
  and in death,
that I may be yours for ever
  and ever.

Prayer for Peace

O God, from whom are holy
desires, right counsels and just
deeds, give to your servants that
peace which the world cannot give;
that we may serve you with our
whole hearts, and live quiet lives
under your protection, free from
the fear of our enemies.
Through Christ our Lord.
Amen.

Prayer in Sickness and Pain

Lord, your will be done; I take this for my sins. I offer up to you my sufferings, together with all that my Saviour has suffered for me; and I beg you, through his sufferings, to have mercy on me. Free me from this illness and pain if you will, and if it be for my good. You love me too much to let me suffer unless it be for my good. Therefore, O Lord, I trust myself to you; do with me as you please. In sickness and in health, I wish to love you always.

Prayer for Chastity

O my God, teach me to love others with the purity of your holy Mother. Give me the grace to resist firmly every temptation to impure thoughts, words or actions. Teach me always to love with generosity and goodness, to respect myself and others in the way I act and to reverence the way that you have given us for the creation of new life.

Prayer in Thanksgiving

My God, from my heart I thank you for them any blessings you have given to me. I thank you for having created and baptised me, and for having placed me in your holy Catholic Church; and for having given me so many graces and mercies through the merits of Jesus Christ. And I thank you, dear Jesus, for having become a little child for my sake, to teach me to be holy and humble like you; and for having died upon the Cross that I might have pardon for my sins and get to heaven. Also I thank you for all your other mercies, most of all for those you have given me today.

Against Temptation

O Jesus, the struggle against temptation is not yet finished. My Jesus, when temptation comes near me, make me strong against it. In the moment of temptation may I always say: "My Jesus, mercy! Mary, help!"

O Jesus, may I lead a good life; may I die a happy death. May I receive you before I die. May I say when I am dying: "Jesus, Mary and Joseph, I give you my heart and my soul".

The Divine Praises

Blessed be God.

Blessed be his holy Name.

Blessed be Jesus Christ,
    true God and true Man.

Blessed be the name of Jesus.

Blessed be his most Sacred Heart.

Blessed be his most
    Precious Blood.

Blessed be Jesus in the most Holy
    Sacrament of the Altar.

Blessed be the Holy Spirit,
    the Paraclete.

Blessed be the great Mother
    of God, Mary most holy.

Blessed be her holy and
    Immaculate Conception.

Blessed be her glorious
Assumption.
Blessed be the name of Mary,
Virgin and Mother.
Blessed be St Joseph,
her spouse most chaste.
Blessed be God in his Angels
and in his Saints.

PRAYING WITH
THE SAINTS

St Alphonsus Liguori

My Jesus,
I believe that you are truly present
in the Most Blessed Sacrament.
I love you above all things,
and I desire to possess you within
     my soul.
Since I am unable now to receive
     you sacramentally,
come at least spiritually
     into my heart.

I embrace you as being
    already there,
and unite myself wholly to you.
Never permit me to be separated
    from you.

St Augustine of Hippo

You have made us for yourself,
and our hearts are restless
until they rest in you, Lord God.

St Benedict

O gracious and holy One,
give us the wisdom to perceive you,
intelligence to understand you,
diligence to seek you,
patience to wait for you,
eyes to behold you,

a heart to meditate upon you,
and a life to proclaim you.

St Catherine Labouré

When I go to the chapel, I put
myself before the good God and
say to Him, 'Lord, here I am, give
me what you wish.' If He gives me
something, I am happy and I thank
Him. If He gives me nothing, I
thank Him still, because I do not
deserve anything more. Then I tell
Him all that comes into my mind.
I tell Him my sorrows and my joys,
and I listen.

St Catherine of Siena

O boundless charity! Just as you gave us yourself, wholly God and wholly man, so you left us all of yourself as food so that while we are pilgrims in this life we might not collapse in our weariness, but be strengthened by you, Heavenly Food.

St Clare of Assisi

Embrace the poor Christ. Look upon Him who became contemptible for you, and follow Him, gaze upon Him, consider Him, contemplate Him. If you suffer with Him, you will reign

with Him; if you weep with Him,
you shall rejoice with Him; if
you die with Him on the Cross
of tribulation, you shall possess
heavenly mansions in the splendour
of the saints, and in the Book of
Life your name shall be called
glorious among men.

St Francis of Assisi

I beseech you to show the greatest
possible reverence and honour to
the most holy Body and Blood of
our Lord Jesus Christ, by whom
all things on earth and in heaven
have been restored to peace and
reconciled to the almighty Father.

St Ignatius Loyola

Teach us, good Lord,
to serve you as you deserve;
to give and not to count the cost;
to fight and not to heed the wounds;
to toil and not to seek for rest;
to labour and not to ask for any
reward, save that of knowing that
we do your will.
Amen.

St John XXIII

Jesus is there, the Prisoner of love.
Whether the tabernacle be poor
or precious, Jesus is always there.
The good parishioner of Ars who
was surprised by his saintly parish

priest, St John Vianney, as he stood silently at the dwelling place of Jesus, his lips not even moving in prayer, replied very simply, 'I look at Him, and I think He looks at me, and this feeds my soul, gives me strength.' So there may be prayer, or even contemplation, in the mere gaze of the eyes.

St John Bosco

Do you want the Lord to give you many graces? Visit Him often. Do you want Him to give you few graces? Visit Him rarely. Do you want the devil to attack you? Visit Jesus rarely in the Blessed

Sacrament. Do you want him to flee from you? Visit Jesus often. Do you want to conquer the devil? Take refuge often at the feet of Jesus. Do you want to be conquered by the devil? Forget about visiting Jesus. My dear ones, the Visit to the Blessed Sacrament is an extremely necessary way to conquer the devil. Therefore go often to visit Jesus and the devil will not come out victorious against you.

St Mary Magdalen dei Pazzi

A friend will visit his friend in the morning to wish him a good day,

in the evening a good night, taking
also an opportunity to converse
with him during the day. In like
manner, make visits to Jesus Christ
in the Blessed Sacrament if your
duties allow. It is especially at the
foot of the altar that one prays well.
In all your visits to our Saviour,
frequently offer His Precious Blood
to the Eternal Father. You will
find these visits very conducive to
increase Divine Love in you.

Blessed Mother Teresa of Calcutta

Nowhere on earth are you more
welcome. Nowhere on earth are

you more loved than by Jesus living and truly present in the Most Blessed Sacrament. The time you spend with Jesus in the Blessed Sacrament is the best time you will spend on earth.

> To me, Jesus is my God,
> Jesus is my spouse.
> Jesus is my Life.
> Jesus is my only Love.
> Jesus is my all in all.
> Jesus is my everything.

Jesus, I love you with my whole heart, with my whole being. I have given Him all, even my sins, and He has espoused me to Himself in tenderness and love. Now and for all my life I am the spouse of my crucified Spouse. Amen.

St Thérèse of Lisieux

Remember that our sweet Jesus is there in the Tabernacle expressly for you and you alone. Remember that He burns with the desire to enter your heart. Do not listen to the enemy. Laugh him to scorn, and go without fear to receive Jesus, the God of peace and of love.

RITE OF EUCHARISTIC EXPOSITION AND BENEDICTION

The service of Benediction developed during the Middle Ages during the Corpus Christi processions in which the Blessed Sacrament was held up for veneration. The service was subsequently used at other times throughout the year as an opportunity to give thanks for the Mass and adore Christ present under the form of bread.

Today, the Church encourages this rite to be celebrated in the context of a longer period of reading, prayer and reflection.

EXPOSITION

First of all, the minister exposes the Blessed Sacrament while a hymn is sung, during which he incenses the Sacrament. The following or another hymn may be chosen.

O salutáris hóstia,
Quæ cæli pandis óstium;
Bella premunt hostília,
Da robur, fer auxílium.
Uni Trinóque Dómino
Sit sempitérna glória,

Qui vitam sine término Nobis donet
in pátria.
Amen.

O saving Victim, opening wide
The gate of heaven to man below
Our foes press on from every side
Thine aid supply,
    thy strength bestow.
To thy great name be
    endless praise
Immortal Godhead, One in Three
O grant us endless length of days
In our true native land with thee.
Amen.

ADORATION

A time for silent prayer, readings from Scripture (eg. pages 17-21), litanies or other prayers (pages 25-33) and hymns (pages 88-93). On some occasions, the Prayer of the Church might be said or sung.

BENEDICTION

Towards the end of the exposition, the priest or deacon goes to the altar, genuflects and kneels. Then this hymn or a suitable alternative is sung, during which the minister incenses the sacrament.

Tantum ergo Sacraméntum
Venerémur cérnui:

Et antíquum documéntum
Novo cedat rítui:
Præstet fides suppleméntum
Sénsuum deféctui.
Genitóri, Genitóque,
Laus et iubilátio.
Salus, honor, virtus quoque
Sit et benedíctio;
Procedénti ab utróque;
Compar sit laudátio.
Amen.

Therefore we, before him bending
This great Sacrament revere
Types and shadow shave their
  ending
for the newer rite is here

Faith, our outward sense befriending
Makes the inward vision clear.
Glory let us give, and blessing
To the Father and the Son
Honour, might, and praise
addressing
While eternal ages run
Ever too his love confessing
Who, from both, with both is one.
Amen.

*The traditional responsory may be
used:*

V. Panem de cælo præstitisti eis
(alleluia)

**R. Omne delectamentum in se
habentem (alleluia)**

V. You gave them bread from heaven (alleluia)

R. Containing in itself all goodness (alleluia)

The minister then says the following prayer (or a suitable alternative)

Lord Jesus Christ,
You gave us the Eucharist
As the memorial of your suffering
    and death.
May our worship of this Sacrament
Of your Body and Blood
Help us to experience the salvation
You won for us
And the peace of the kingdom
Where you live with the Father

And the Holy Spirit,
One God, for ever and ever.
Amen.

*The priest or deacon now puts
on the humeral veil and blesses
the congregation with the Blessed
Sacrament.*

*The Divine Praises (page 32)
formerly said at this point may
more properly be included within
the period of adoration.*

REPOSITION

*Immediately after the Blessed
Sacrament is reposed in the
tabernacle, the following may be
sung:*

Ant. Adorémus in ætérnum
sanctíssimum Sacraméntum.

Ps. Laudáte Dóminum, omnes
gentes; laudáte eum omnes pópuli.
Quóniam confirmáta est super nos
misericórdia ejus; et véritas Dómini
manet in ætérnum.

Glória Patri, et Filio, et Spirítui
Sancto. Sicut erat in princípio,
et nunc, et semper, et in sáecula
sæculórum. **Amen.**

Ant. Adorémus in ætérnum
sanctíssimum Sacraméntum.

Ant. Let us adore for ever the most holy Sacrament.

Ps. O praise the Lord, all you nations
Acclaim him, all you peoples
For his mercy is confirmed upon us
and the truth of the Lord
    remains for ever.

Glory be to the Father, and to the Son
and to the Holy Spirit
As it was in the beginning, is now
and ever shall be,
    world without end. **Amen.**

Ant. Let us adore for ever the most holy Sacrament.

ROSARY MEDITATIONS BEFORE THE BLESSED SACRAMENT

Contemplate the beauty of Christ with Mary

With Mary, we will understand better the transforming power of the Eucharist. By listening to her, we will find in the Eucharistic mystery the courage and energy to follow Christ, the Good Shepherd, and to serve him in the brethren.

The Mysteries of the Rosary

Traditionally, different Mysteries of the Rosary are said on different days of the week.

The Joyful Mysteries
 - *Mondays, Saturdays*
The Luminous Mysteries
 - *Thursdays*
The Sorrowful Mysteries
 - *Tuesdays, Fridays*
The Glorious Mysteries
 - *Wednesdays, Sundays*

We begin by saying the Creed:

The Prayers of the Rosary

I believe in God, the Father almighty, Creator of heaven and earth, and in Jesus Christ, his only Son, our Lord, who was conceived by the Holy Spirit, born of the Virgin Mary, suffered under Pontius Pilate, was crucified, died and was buried; he descended into hell; on the third day he rose again from the dead; he ascended into heaven, and is seated at the right hand of God the Father almighty; from there he will come to judge the living and the dead. I believe in the Holy Spirit, the holy catholic Church, the communion of saints, the forgiveness of sins, the resurrection of the body, and life everlasting. **Amen.**

At the end of the Rosary we say:

Hail, holy Queen, mother of mercy; hail, our life, our sweetness, and our hope! To you do we cry, poor banished children of Eve; to you do we send up our sighs, mourning and weeping in this vale of tears. Turn then, most gracious advocate, your eyes of mercy towards us; and after this our exile, show to us the blessed fruit of your womb, Jesus. O clement, O loving, O sweet Virgin Mary.

V. Pray for us, O holy Mother of God.

R. That we may be made worthy of the promises of Christ.

Let us pray.

O God, whose only-begotten Son, by his life, death and resurrection, has purchased for us the rewards of eternal life; grant, we beseech you, that meditating on these Mysteries of the most holy Rosary of the Blessed Virgin Mary, we may both imitate what they contain, and obtain what they promise, through the same Christ our Lord.

Amen.

THE JOYFUL MYSTERIES

The First Joyful Mystery

The Annunciation and the Holy Eucharist

Behold the handmaid of the Lord: let it be done to me according to your word. (*Lk* 1:38)

The Holy Eucharist is the extension of the Mystery of the Incarnation. When Mary said "let it be done to me according to your word", then the Incarnation took place. When the priest says in Mass "this is my Body" and "this is my Blood", Jesus himself is made present in the Eucharistic elements.

Intention: That we may always make a worthy communion.

The Second Joyful Mystery

The Visitation and the Holy Eucharist

Mary arose and went with haste into the hill country. (*Lk* 1:39)

Mary carries Jesus secretly in her womb along a hurried journey, a journey of corporal and spiritual mercy.

The Blessed Sacrament is carried by priests and ministers of the Eucharist on journeys of corporal and spiritual mercy. The sick restored to health and the dying strengthened and comforted and the good news of salvation is proclaimed.

Intention: We remember those who cannot get to Mass.

The Third Joyful Mystery

The Nativity and the Holy Eucharist

She wrapped him in swaddling clothes and laid him in a manger because there was no room for them at the inn. (Lk 2:7)

Jesus is born in poverty and cold, in a stable on a winter's night.

Jesus comes to us at Mass
in poverty. The scoffing of
unbelievers, the indifference of the
lukewarm and those who receive
communion unworthily is surely
more painful to him than the cold
of the stable at Bethlehem.

As in the stable, so in the
Blessed Sacrament, the angels,
the shepherds and the poor adore
him while to the world he remains
unknown.

Intention: That we may set our
hearts on Christ and not on this
world.

The Fourth Joyful Mystery

The Presentation and the Holy Eucharist

My eyes have seen the salvation which you have prepared before the face of all peoples. (*Lk* 2:30)

At the Presentation in the Temple, Simeon, who had looked forward to the consolation of Israel, at last received Jesus as his Viaticum. In the Blessed Sacrament, Jesus is the Viaticum of dying Catholics.

How many faithful Christians on the threshold of eternity are embracing Jesus for the last time on earth, with hearts overflowing with gratitude, breathing their own "Nunc dimittis!"

Intention: That we may have a holy death.

The Fifth Joyful Mystery

The Finding of the young Jesus in the Temple and the Holy Eucharist

Did you not know that I must be about my Father's business?
(*Lk* 2:49)

After losing Jesus for three days - a time of spiritual darkness and heart-breaking sorrow - Mary and Joseph find him in the Temple, listening and asking questions. What rapture of joy to find him again!

How many of us, after losing Jesus by sin or in the desolation of spiritual darkness find him again when we celebrate the Eucharist? He finds us and makes his dwelling with us, in the Temple that is our own mortal body.

Intention: That we may constantly seek the Lord.

THE LUMINOUS MYSTERIES

The First Luminous Mystery

Christ's Baptism and the Holy Eucharist

He saw the heavens open and the Spirit descending upon him like a dove. (*Mk* 1:10)

The sacraments of the Church are effective signs and means of our salvation, the ordinary is transformed into the extraordinary through the action of the Holy Spirit. At Mass, the priest invokes the Holy Spirit: "Let your Spirit come down on these gifts to make them holy, so that they may become for us the body and blood of our Lord Jesus Christ."

Intention: That we may have greater awareness of the Holy Spirit.

The Second Luminous Mystery

Christ's self-revelation at the wedding of Cana and the Holy Eucharist

His mother said to the servants "Do whatever he tells you. (Jn 2:5)

Christ reveals his glory by changing the water into wine, after which his disciples believed in him.

Likewise in the Eucharist, Christ's glory is hidden in the form of bread and wine. In countless churches and chapels, Christ's Eucharistic glory is adored by those who see with faith, while the world outside carries on muchas before.

Intention: That we may have a faith like Mary's.

The Third Luminous Mystery

Christ's proclamation of the Kingdom of God and the Holy Eucharist

The time is fulfilled and the kingdom

*of God is at hand. Repent and
believe in the good news.* (*Mk* 1:15)

Jesus' proclamation of the kingdom
of God is made real not just by
words but by his actions. His very
words bring about the reality they
signify: healing the sick and
the lame.

At Mass, the very words of
consecration bring about the
transformation of bread and wine

As Christ's Eucharistic presence
is real and efficacious, so is his
forgiveness.

Intention: We pray to have hearts
that listen to the voice of the Lord.

The Fourth Luminous Mystery

The Transfiguration and the Holy Eucharist

They lifted up their eyes, and saw no one but Jesus. (*Mt* 17:8)

Jesus takes Peter, James and John up a high mountain, where "his face shone like the sun and his garments became white as light." Moses and Elijah appear with Jesus, representing the Law and the prophets.

The Eucharist is a fulfilment of the promises of the old covenant.

When we celebrate the Eucharist, we commemorate Christ's paschal victory and the liberation from the slavery of sin he won for us. Truly the table of the Lord is the holy mountain!

Intention: We pray for greater attention at Mass.

The Fifth Luminous Mystery

The Institution of the Holy Eucharist

I tell you I shall not drink again of the fruit of the vine until that day when I drink it anew with you in my Father's kingdom. (Mt 26:29)

The Eucharist is but a foretaste of the heavenly banquet which Christ has prepared for those who love him, when all the tribes will be gathered up, when every tear will be wiped away. We look back with remembrance to the upper room, we look forward in hope to the Father's house.

Intention: That we may long for the food which lasts.

THE SORROWFUL MYSTERIES

The First Sorrowful Mystery

The Agony in the Garden and the Holy Eucharist

His sweat became like great drops of blood. (*Lk* 22:44)

Imagine the sanctuary of a church as the garden of the Christian soul. Jesus calls his disciples to be with him, to watch and pray.

Though the spirit is willing, the flesh is weak. Some fall asleep. Some even come into his presence and betray him with a kiss, and deliver him into the hands of sinners.

Intention: That we may have a humble heart and a contrite spirit.

The Second Sorrowful Mystery

The Scourging at the Pillar and the Holy Eucharist

Pilate took Jesus and had him scourged. (*Jn* 19:1)

In the mystery of the Eucharist, Jesus has bound himself to the consecrated species of bread and wine, as it were to a pillar, to be scourged by the ingratitude of men and women.

The forgetfulness of believers and the sneers of unbelievers and sceptics are an endless scourge to the love of Jesus in the Blessed Sacrament.

Intention: May we be ever conscious of our sins and their consequences.

The Third Sorrowful Mystery

The Crowning with thorns and the Holy Eucharist

Kneeling before him they mocked him. (*Mt* 27:29)

In the Blessed Sacrament we place Jesus on a throne and ask for his blessing. We bend the knee and adore him. But how do the royal honours we pay him appear in the sight of angels who veil their faces in his presence.

It is too often mere formality. And when we receive communion without gratitude, is not our indifference worse than the sneers and spittle of brutal soldiers.

Intention: That we may have great reverence for the Blessed Sacrament.

The Fourth
Sorrowful Mystery

The Carrying of the Cross
and the Holy Eucharist

*Carrying his own cross he went out
to the Place of the Skull.* (*Jn* 19:18)

In the Blessed Sacrament Jesus
makes each one's cross his own.
Nothing raises the soul above
the sorrows, disappointments
and sufferings of life like Holy
Communion. Jesus, who carried
the weight of the cross to Calvary
assures us that "my yoke is easy
and my burden light."

Intention: That we may be patient in tribulation.

The Fifth Sorrowful Mystery

The Crucifixion and the Holy Eucharist

Father, into your hands I commend my spirit. (*Lk* 23:46)

The very same sacrifice which took place on the Cross is mystically and sacramentally made present at the celebration of the Eucharist. Like those at the foot of the cross so are we brought into ever closer communion by the mystery we celebrate.

"As often as you eat this bread and drink this cup, you proclaim the Lord's death until he comes in glory." (*1 Cor* 11:26)

Intention: That we may love God above all else and our neighbour as ourself.

THE GLORIOUS MYSTERIES

The First Glorious Mystery

The Resurrection and the Holy Eucharist

He is going before you to Galilee, there you will see him. (*Mk* 16:7)

Holy Communion is the pledge of the Resurrection to everlasting life. "The one who eats my flesh and drinks my blood has eternal life, and I will raise him up on the last day." (*Jn* 6:54)

The life of Jesus in the Blessed Sacrament is a kind of continuation of the forty days after the

Resurrection. His human nature - now glorified - is immortal; hidden yet intimately present.

Intention: We pray for joy in Christ's sacramental presence.

The Second Glorious Mystery

The Ascension and the Holy Eucharist

He was taken up to heaven and sat down at the right hand of God. (*Mk* 16:19)

That same Jesus whom we adore in the Blessed Sacrament has been on the throne of God since the Ascension, pronouncing judgement. "Before him will be gathered all the nations, and he will separate them one from another as a shepherd separates the sheep from the goats." (*Mt* 25:32)

Intention: We pray for confidence in the love of God for us.

The Third Glorious Mystery

The Descent of the Holy Spirit and the Holy Eucharist

They were all filled with the Holy Spirit and began to speak in other tongues. (*Ac* 2:4)

The Holy Spirit who conceived Jesus in the womb of the Virgin

Mary today conceives him in the hearts of those who believe. That same Spirit prepares every soul to receive Christ at Holy Communion.

It is the Spirit who inspires the contrition, the faith, hope and love that makes the poor sinner worthy to receive Jesus.

Intention: We pray for zeal to spread the Gospel.

The Fourth Glorious Mystery

The Assumption of our Lady and the Holy Eucharist

If I go and prepare a place for you, I will come back and take you with me so that you also may be where I am. (*Jn* 14:3)

The Assumption was the completion of Mary's life-long communion with Jesus. She had always given hospitality to Jesus in her soul. Mary dwelt in Jesus and he in her. That is what Holy Communion is. By her Assumption into heaven, the earthly union of Jesus and his mother matured, was consummated and sealed for eternity in glory.

Intention: We remember all those who have died.

The Fifth Glorious Mystery

The Crowning of our Lady and the Holy Eucharist

A great sign appeared in heaven: a woman, adorned with the sun, standing on the moon, and with the twelve stars on her head for a crown. (Rv 12:1)

When crowned by her Divine Son, Mary is made Queen of the mystical Body of Christ - the Church. She is Mother of the body and blood, the principal bond which unites its members to each other and to Christ.

This is a glorious fulfilment of the words uttered in the darkest hour of the Passion: "Woman, behold your son." Now in the eternal glory of heaven she does indeed behold her Son.

Intention: That our longing for heaven and eternal life may always increase.

HYMNS AND POEMS

Sweet Sacrament Divine

Sweet Sacrament divine,
Hid in thine earthly home;
Lo! round thy lowly shrine,
With suppliant hearts we come;
Jesus, to thee our voice we raise
In songs of love and heartfelt praise
Sweet Sacrament divine.

Sweet Sacrament of peace,
Dear home of every heart,
Where restless yearnings cease,
And sorrows all depart.

There in thine ear, all trustfully, We
tell our tale of misery,
Sweet Sacrament of peace.

Sweet Sacrament of rest,
Ark from the ocean's roar,
Within thy shelter blest
Soon may we reach the shore;
Save us, for still the tempest raves,
Save, lest we sink beneath the
waves: Sweet Sacrament of rest.

Sweet Sacrament divine,
Earth's light and jubilee,
In thy far depths doth shine
The Godhead's majesty;
Sweet light, so shine on us, we pray

That earthly joys may fade away:
Sweet Sacrament divine.

(Francis Stanfield)

Bless the Lord

Bless the Lord, my soul,
and bless his holy name.
Bless the Lord, my soul,
he rescues me from death.

(Taizé)

I need thee every hour

I need thee every hour,
    most gracious Lord;
No tender voice like thine
    can peace afford.

I need thee, O I need thee;
Every hour I need thee;

O bless me now, my Saviour,
I come to thee.

I need thee every hour,
    stay thou nearby;
Temptations lose their power
    when thou art nigh.

I need thee every hour,
    in joy or pain;
Come quickly and abide,
    or life is in vain.

I need thee every hour;
    teach me thy will;
And thy rich promises
    in me fulfill.

I need thee every hour,
most Holy One;
O make me thine indeed,
thou blessèd Son.

(*Annie S. Hawkes*)

Soul of my Saviour
Soul of my Saviour sanctify
my breast,
Body of Christ,
be thou my saving guest,
Blood of my Saviour,
bathe me in thy tide,
wash me with waters
gushing from thy side.

Strength and protection may thy
    passion be,
O blessèd Jesus,
    hear and answer me;
Deep in thy wounds,
    Lord, hide and shelter me,
So shall I never,
    never part from thee.
Guard and defend me from
    the foe malign,
In death's dread moments
    make me only thine;
Call me and bid me come to thee
    on high
Where I may praise thee with thy
    saints for ay.

    (Traditionally ascribed to John XXII)

All rights reserved. Published 2014 by the Incorporated Catholic Truth Society, 40-46 Harleyford Road, London SE11 5AY. Tel: 020 7640 0042 Fax 020 7640 0046. website:www.CTSbooks. org. Copyright © 2014, first published 2014 by The Incorporated Catholic Truth Society, all rights reserved.

ISBN 978 1 86082 924 6

CTS gratefully acknowledges the editorial contributions of Fr Peter Edwards, Fr Richard Rutt, Mr Adrian Thacker and Mr Barry Midgely towards this volume.

CTS gratefully acknowledges use of Holy Communion and Worship of the Eucharist Outside Mass (The Roman Ritual) Vol. 1 Rites, Vol. II Biblical Readings. Approved by the Bishops' Conferences of England & Wales, Ireland and Scotland, and Confirmed by Decrees of the Sacred Congregation for the Sacraments and Divine Worship 29th May 1976.

For those quotations for which we have been unable to trace the copyright holder, the Publisher would be grateful to receive any information as to their identity